THE REMAINS OF BURNING
Therapeutic Journal

POETRY AND WRITING PROMPTS
TO PROCESS PAIN AND LOSS.

Lauren Lott

Copyright © 2022 Lauren Lott
All rights reserved.
No part of this book may be used or reproduced in any manner
without written permission by the author.
ISBN:978-0-6489466-5-6

I sat across from an Italian emissary
this is what he told me.
'Write. Let your tears become
the waters that refresh others.'

Therapeutic Writing Guidelines

Research shows therapeutic writing strengthens mental, emotional, and physical health by reducing stress, regulating emotions, boosting memory and improving overall wellbeing.

Before journalling consider the guidelines below.

1. Keep this journal private. It is hard to commit to honesty if you know someone will read what you have wriiten. For this reason, it is best to journal alone.

2. Don't judge yourself for feeling certain emotions. All feeling is welcome on the page, and has its place in your life.

3. Take time to observe your emotions by re-reading what you have wriiten. This will allow you to make sense of what you have been through.

4. Assess your needs and become more aware of your innermost thoughts and feelings by using this journal regualrly.

5. If a certain poem or prompt stirs up excessive distress, take a break or leave it for another time.

6. Understand, writing for therapeutic purposes is deep work. You may feel strong emotion. Do not plan anything emotionally or cognitively taxing after writing.

7. I have included a small section at the back of the journal for you to write notes. This is a good place to write down your

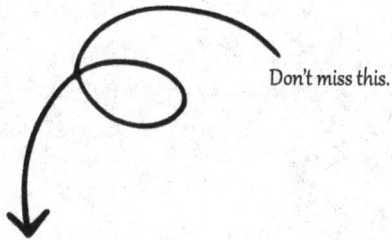
Don't miss this.

BEFORE YOU START
Find a quiet place. Minimise distractions.
Surround yourself with sounds and scents you
find relaxing. Choose your favourite pen.
Pour yourself a glass of water or make yourself
a hot beverage. Get comfortable.
Exhale slowly and begin.

The Snatch Of Flame.

The Remains of Burning Therapeutic Journal

First, hold your breath.
For disbelief swells high,
and to survive, you must deep dive,
and hope when you rise,
you will remember how to breathe.
For breathing is all you will be able
to do for a while.

-upon hearing the news.

Lauren Lott

In the space below, try to express in words, what you thought and felt when you first heard unexpected life-changing news.

The Remains of Burning Therapeutic Journal

We, each in our beds,
nursing our hearts,
trying to breathe.
We must remember,
our pain is not unique.
It belongs to all on the night watch.
And so, I think of you,
feeling as I do,
and I hope you think of me,
though you have never seen my face.

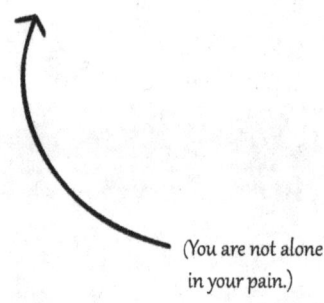

(You are not alone
in your pain.)

Lauren Lott

Emotional pain can make you feel isolated and lonely. Knowing that your pain is not unique, that there are other people experiencing the same kind of suffering, can help. In the space below, write what you would say to someone who is feeling what you feel now.

The Remains of Burning Therapeutic Journal

> Pain is a crier;
> a personal bellman.
> He comes to awaken truth;
> to show what is shakable,
> and what is sure.
> What comes and goes as a flame,
> and what remains.

Lauren Lott

What or who has proven to be strong and reliable during this painful season?

The Remains of Burning Therapeutic Journal

We deliver
lost dreams
one limb at a time;
wiping up the evidence
of decomposing desires
month after month.
Though the stench
of what used to live
in the womb of our heart
lingers not forever,
there are little graves
everywhere.

(Places and dates and songs and food and actually any everyday random things can trigger memories and make you feel sad or angry or hurt.)

Lauren Lott

Loss touches more than one aspect of our lives. Write down how loss has influenced not only your thoughts, emotions and physical wellbeing, but also your relationships, finances and future goals.

The Remains of Burning Therapeutic Journal

Lonely heart
unforgotten,
take peace and
wrap it blanket-tight,
or use it to cover your ears,
so you cannot hear
those tall stories that tower,
and tell you
you've been left behind.
You have not been cast aside,
but repositioned,
picked out for something
rare and meaningful.

Lauren Lott

What stories do you need to silence?

Pain sometimes sends a message of defeat and dire straits, causing us to believe that life can never be good again. In the space below, write a few words you wish to believe about your situation, that will give you some hope.

The Remains of Burning Therapeutic Journal

Maybe this pain is mercy.
Saving us from the shallows,
keeping us for tomorrows,
intentionally piercing our skin,
carefully knitting on wings.

Lauren Lott

Though you may feel weak, how is grief strengthening you?

(This is a hard one. Skip it for now if you are not ready to answer.)

The Remains of Burning Therapeutic Journal

Though you feel like dirt.
Disposable.
Disgraced.
Stripped of dignity.
Underserving of love.
You are worth,
the stars,
the moon,
the sea,
the earth.

-don't let the pain fool you.

Pain can make you feel worthless. It can fool you into believing you are not enough. Write down any untruths that your pain is telling you.

(It's time to shine a light on all the lies you have been lead to believe about what you don't deserve and how you don't measure up. Write without fear!)

The Remains of Burning Therapeutic Journal

What happened there
gave us new eyes,
and a heart for ones
we did not see before.

-pop goes the bubble.

Lauren Lott

After experiencing intense pain, how has your perspective changed?

How has pain cultivated in you empathy for others?
Who do you see now, that you didn't see before this hard season?

Now and then,
life shifts to show
us our strength,
and who is strong for us.

-only those who are free came running.

Who has proven to be the most supportive during this season of loss? Write down the words or gestures that have meant the most to you?

The Remains of Burning Therapeutic Journal

Revolution starts within,
and pain is usually the instigator.

-the beginning feels like the end.

(Your pain is not meaningless.)

Pain may try to provoke you to do what you would not normally do. How can you turn this into a positive in your life?

It is ok to spend the day crying;
it is the work that needs doing.
You've got to feel it
before you can free it.

(Crying is a way you
can self-soothe.
It helps improve sleep
and detoxifies the body.)

Lauren Lott

Processing emotional pain is important work. Honour your healing by creating space to feel real emotion. Write down ways that you might be avoiding processing pain. How can you give yourself space to grieve well?

The Remains of Burning Therapeutic Journal

Look at her.
Look at how she still pushes
hope in and out of her lungs.

-breathing is a badge of honour.

Lauren Lott

Sometimes, simply still being here is a win.
Write an encouraging message to yourself that celebrates seemingly small victories that are really important.

The Remains of Burning Therapeutic Journal

Today is one of those days,
you know the kind when you must
muster up every ounce of courage your
frightened heart can find.

-letting go of us.

Lauren Lott

Do you feel forced to let go of things you want to hold?
What emotions arise when you think about having to live
with circumstances you didn't choose?

(Go on, write something really honest.)

The Remains of Burning Therapeutic Journal

One cannot simply
walk into the wilderness.
It is a place for the kidnapped;
those awakened by night,
and taken from their comfy beds.
Many will report them missing;
they are not where they used to be,
but it will soon be seen,
that the wild is where
we are all meant to be.

Lauren Lott

How has experiencing loss changed you? List the changes you see in yourself.

The Remains of Burning Therapeutic Journal

Day asked night,
'What is a broken heart?'
Night answered day,
'When you discover your people,
 are not your people.'

-detours are for picking up new friends.

(Being rejected, abandoned,
negelected, or beytrayed
by those we trust wounds
us deeply. When this happes,
it is normal to feel
lost, confussed and unsure
of what is real)

Lauren Lott

In the space below, write how pain and loss has changed your relationships. Who do you wish to farewell? Who do you wish to bring closer?

The Remains of Burning Therapeutic Journal

Tell the clouds,
my darling.
Send it up
and let it turn to rain.

-what to do with the other side of the story.

Sometimes, to add to suffering, our story is silenced. This is often only benefits those who did you wrong. To heal, it is important to tell your side of the story. Name someone you can trust to listen and be a compassionate witness to your version of events? When and how will you share your story?

The Cooling of Coals.

The Remains of Burning Therapeutic Journal

I thought possibility
clothed herself in colour;
orchid purple,
pear green,
ocean blue.
Now I see,
she wears sackcloth
and sits in ashes.

Lauren Lott

What new possibilities has pain and loss presented to you?

The Remains of Burning Therapeutic Journal

Here begins the raking of ashes,
and I am forced to farewell
that which has long been a part of me.
All I can keep is what the truth fire
did not burn up.

*(Pain has a way of unmasking us.
We discover that we have less
tolerance for niceties or dramatics.)*

Lauren Lott

How has pain and loss helped you to live in greater truth?

I waited for others
to empower me,
not knowing
it is the work of ashes,
not knowing
that the cooling of coals,
is the coming of courage.

-the making of me.

Lauren Lott

How has pain empowered you? What responsibilities are you taking back? How has pain made you more courageous?

The Remains of Burning Therapeutic Journal

I understand,
you want to go back,
but even if you could
it would not be as good as it was,
or as fitting as it could have been before
everything changed.

-places become ghosts too.

Lauren Lott

Write down any physical/geographical places you miss. Are there any places or spaces that once felt like home but now feel forereign?

(It's ok to create new boundaries. You do not have to return to unsafe places. Give up the idea that returning will restore you.)

The Remains of Burning Therapeutic Journal

Stop and say,
'This is where I am.
All these lessons are mine.
The seat in the shade is mine.
The view of the valley is mine.
The pang in my heart is mine.
They are all my teachers.'

Lauren Lott

Write your own version of the poem on page 50.

The _____ is mine.

The _____ is mine.

The _____ is mine.

_____ is my teacher.

(Remember, when writing for therapeutic purposes, it doesn't have to make sense to anyone but you.)

Identify an unexpected 'teacher' that has helped you learn through adversity.

The Remains of Burning Therapeutic Journal

> Peace now,
> It's only the exhale;
> the learning.

In the space below, make a list of ways you can hold your peace. It may be as simple as deleting your social platforms or changing your schedule.

The Remains of Burning Therapeutic Journal

You cannot speed up the moon,
or ease the hours before dawn;
the night is for holding on.
Wait, and let darkness work on you.

*(It sounds painful,
but between the falling
and the rising is where
the magic happens.
You are germinating!)*

Pain can cause you to look for an escape. Drugs, alcohol, sex, sleep and shopping are just some of the things people use to try and relieve pain. Can you identify anything you are using to escape that could be harmful?

What boundaries can you put into place to protect yourself and others from unhealthy or even dangerous habits?

The Remains of Burning Therapeutic Journal

Life is what you do with
the 'could have been'.

Lauren Lott

With loss comes disappointment. Disappointment can reveal unhealthy attachments and real connections. Write down what disappointment has shown you.

The Remains of Burning Therapeutic Journal

(This question might be
difficult to answer
if you have never thought
about it before.)

Quiet now,
you don't have
to fulfil expectations;
not even your own.

Write down three expectations you have of yourself.

In what ways, if any, do you feel like you have not met these expectations?

The Remains of Burning Therapeutic Journal

I asked for you,
but you would not come.
I don't know if it was your pride,
or angels intervening,
knowing what they know,
seeing as they do.

-praying for storms.

Lauren Lott

Can you recall a time when you wanted something and it turned out good that you didn't get it. Write about it in the space below.

The Remains of Burning Therapeutic Journal

This is what
you are made to do,
unfold in love,
continue to be renewed.
And when you move
not all will move too,
but it is well,
this is your breakthrough.

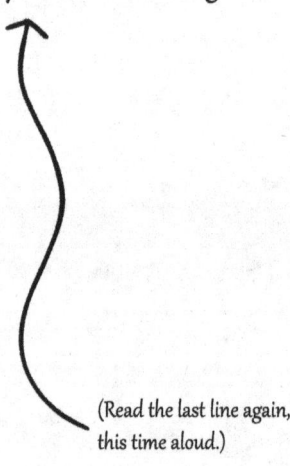

(Read the last line again,
this time aloud.)

Lauren Lott

Growth can be lonely. Growth can make you feel unknown. How has your growth changed your relationships?

The Remains of Burning Therapeutic Journal

We know about the falling,
because we celebrate the rising,
but between them lives hours and hours
of wading through ashes.
Days of sitting with surrender.
Nobody likes to talk about that.

-silent Saturdays.

Often processing pain and loss takes longer than you would like. Write about how it feels to live between the falling and rising.

The Remains of Burning Therapeutic Journal

> You can't outrun a storm.
> You can't tame thunder.
> Just be still,
> be still in it.

-secret powers.

(What are you afraid of?)

Write down how you can make more time to practice stillness in your life.

What do you find most challenging about taking time to be still and silent?

The Remains of Burning Therapeutic Journal

I gazed at stars
until the darkness
became beautiful,
and being on the outside
felt like home.

Lauren Lott

Write about the beauty you found through suffering. What do you appreciate now that you did not appreciate before you experienced pain?

The Remains of Burning Therapeutic Journal

> This place is sacred.
> For under these
> stain glass skies,
> I am surviving.
> That is the miracle of me.

(Don't diminish your experiences. It is amazing that you are still here allowing yourself to heal.)

Lauren Lott

You have endured a lot. Write a list of what you have survived in celebration of yourself and those who have helped you.

The Remains of Burning Therapeutic Journal

I spent time wondering
how you sleep at night.
Then it came to me.
You've never been awake.
You're a sleepwalker,
lost in your story.

-bliss.

Write about how the pain opened your eyes to see what you may have been ignorant of in the past.

Knowing that everyone is ignorant of something, how does that change the way you see those who have caused you pain?

The Remains of Burning Therapeutic Journal

Deal with it
before it deals you the life
you never wanted.

-forgive or die trying.

Lauren Lott

Forgiveness is difficult yet imperitive to your health and freedom. Write how you can nurture forgiveness in your heart.

The Remains of Burning Therapeutic Journal

We are more than what
we hold in our hands;
what we perceive
with our senses.
The shaking told me so.

-lessons from the bathroom floor.

Prior to your suffering, what are some misconceptions you had about yourself.

(Misconception means false beliefs, delusions, wrong ideas.)

Answers do not heal,
unlike time and beauty,
and they are always with you.

In the space below, write down some things that have not changed through your suffering.

List 3 things of beauty that are still in your life.

1.

2.

3.

The Remains of Burning Therapeutic Journal

Do not grieve today,
what is for tomorrow.
We hear the storm
before we drink the rain.

Lauren Lott

Sometimes we are too quick to welcome disappointment. Don't underestimate the good things that can come into your life. What are you waiting for?

What are you watching for?

The Remains of Burning Therapeutic Journal

And I run deeper
into the wilderness,
further from what is known,
to find who lives there,
and what lives in me.
And the only time I rest,
is to name the past
or settle the future;
to bless what is
and what will never be.

Lauren Lott

Naming the past means calling the past what it was and leaving it there. Settling the future means deciding that whatever the future holds, you will have what you need to deal with it when it comes.

Complete these sentences.

I am ok dispite...

I will be ok even if...

The Remains of Burning Therapeutic Journal

We are here to be wildlings;
to master thievery
and ravage the wasteland.
Every thorn belongs to us.
They are our trials,
our pains,
and we will use them
to prick our skin,
creating holes
where liberty can pour in.

(For the sake of freedom
press into your pain and
let it make you stronger,
braver, kinder, wiser.)

What has pain freed you from? Write about all the ways you have become uninhibited.

What is something you once tresured that is no longer important?

The Remains of Burning Therapeutic Journal

They say I must let go of the old,
before I can take hold of the new.
But what if it's a trick?
What if I am left empty-handed?
Still, I am suspicious of love;
I believe it has something up its sleeve.
This is how I surrender.
This is how I am strong.

Being postive about the future helps us to surrender to the present. Imagine for a moment that you could use your pain to create something for others. What would it be?

What can you do to help make this a reality?

The Remains of Burning Therapeutic Journal

There will always be disappointment.
Things hoped for but never held:
the cancellation of plans,
the breaking of promises,
the turning of hearts.
But through it all,
and though we cry,
there is beauty,
there is music,
there is love.

Lauren Lott

Rewrite the end of the poem on page 88 by filling in the blank spaces.

But through it all and though I cry,

there is...

there is...

there is...

How can you exerience more of what is good about life everyday?

(Scheduling things you enjoy is a way you can infuse joy into your day. You can carry grief and joy together.)

The Remains of Burning Therapeutic Journal

Think love.
Think love.
Think love, my love.
This is your power;
the only way to be free.

-what the healers, the healed and the healing know.

Thinking loving thoughts sets us free. Sending good will to those who have not been good to us releases us from their control. Name three people you want to wish well.

How does it feel to know you are empowered to free yourself by choosing to love others?

# The Value Of Ashes.

The Remains of Burning Therapeutic Journal

Although I am
a little blistered,
a little bruised,
the breaking
put a part of me
back together.

Lauren Lott

Can you relate to this poem? Write what it means to you.

The Remains of Burning Therapeutic Journal

And if the day
has brought you pain,
or been ruined by bad news,
finish it with kindness.
Hold your body.
Quiet your heart.
Turn your mind
from hurtful thoughts.
For not a day is wasted
when love is at work.

Lauren Lott

It's important to love and respect yourself.
In the space below, write a list of ways you can show yourself kindness.

Beauty
helped
to make
it better.

-in heart and mind.

Being in beautiful places can assist your healing.
Being aware of what you look at, listen to and think about can have a real effect on life. Below, list 5 beautiful things that help to sooth your emotional pain.

1.

2.

3.

4.

5.

These ashes tell the story of us;
they speak of the past
and a possible future.

-rebuilding needs ruins.

How will you rebuild the parts of life that have been effected by pain and loss? Is ther anything you feel can not be rebuilt?

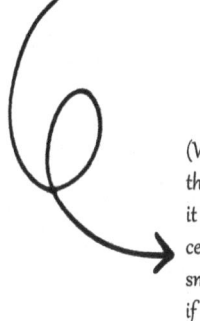

(When we loose someone that can not be replaced, it may be a comfort to celebrate in your own small way, that you had, if only for a short time, the honor and liberty to behold them.)

The Remains of Burning Therapeutic Journal

I am grateful
for locked doors.
They taught me
to walk down hallways,
and out into the vast and beautiful.

cheers to the outsiders.

(After feeling the pain of rejection, outsiders often discover the beauty and freedom found in not fitting in.)

Lauren Lott

What good experiences/opportunities emerged after loss? How has loss directed you away from things/people that are not right for you?

The Remains of Burning Therapeutic Journal

Dear comfort,
I'm coming for you.
Kind regards,
Freedom.

Sometimes we can think we are free, but in truth, we are just comfortable. How has suffering decreased comfort but increased freedom?

What fear has your suffering helped you to conquer?

The Remains of Burning Therapeutic Journal

The state of my heart.
The span of my wings.
The depth of my unknowing.
The fragility of my certainties.
The strength of my spirit.

-things I did not know until I witnessed the wild place.

List five things you did not know about yourself until you experienced deep emotional pain?

1.

2.

3.

4.

5.

Which of the five things listed above are you most proud of?

The Remains of Burning Therapeutic Journal

I hope you know
the value of ashes,
and do not let them
be stolen by the breeze.
But use them to
build great cities of glory,
to write resurrection stories,
and make monuments
to what you believe.

Lauren Lott

Take what has happend in your life and build something beautiful. What could you do to amplify
the story of your healing?

The Remains of Burning Therapeutic Journal

Love is in yesterday;
in the hour I saw you last.
Love is present here,
though I don't always sense
the many ways you come to me.
Love is in tomorrow,
preparing rooms and hearts to walk into.
Love is in it all:
the blur of memories,
the breath of certainties,
the blink of possibilities.

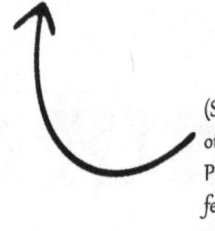

(Showing love and compassion to others is hard when you are hurt. Projecting your pain might feel like the only way to gain some releif. However, practicing compassion and kindness is a way to improve your mood and welbeing.)

Write down a loving memory.

Write down how love is evident at the present time.

Write down what you can do to show love to someone you plan to see in the future.

The Remains of Burning Therapeutic Journal

When pain becomes wings.

-my favourite season.

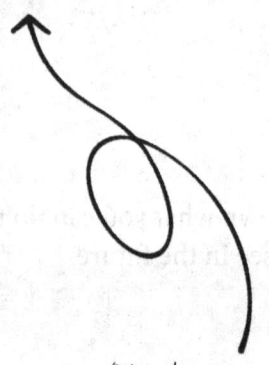

(Winged creatures are sometimes seen as a symbol of freedom.)

Lauren Lott

There will come a time when pain can be used to elevate your life and the lives of others. Who do you know that has proven this to be true? What do you admire about them?

Each morning says
the same thing,
'Look ahead.'

-the hardest thing on my 'to do' list.

Write down five things you are grateful for now.

1.

2.

3.

4.

5.

Write down what you are looking forward to in the future.

The Remains of Burning Therapeutic Journal

Mostly I am too busy for mystery.
But when I stop,
oh, when I stop,
the silence sings a mighty chorus,
and I sense that something
magnificent is going on.

Lauren Lott

Stop and be silent. What do you see?

What do you hear?

What do you feel?

What is your heart telling you?

The Remains of Burning Therapeutic Journal

Why wrestle for room in the nest
when all the wild is yours?

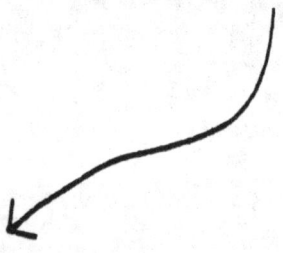

(It can be hard to find your place inside
the world in which you lived prior to your
experience. Often the nest (home, job,
relationship) must be surrendered so you
can make room for what your experience
has taught you.)

Lauren Lott

What are you curious about?

Where or what do you wish to explore?

The Remains of Burning Therapeutic Journal

These four words
we long to say and mean.
'It was worth it.'
All the toiling and tears.
All the days, months and years
gave us gold;
if not in our pockets,
then in our hearts.

Lauren Lott

How has experience, both good and bad, made you rich in courage, compassion and wisdom?

The Remains of Burning Therapeutic Journal

Draw a heart around it,
and colour it in.

-how I fix mistakes on the page and in the past.

(Like this!)

Lauren Lott

Write a few words to your past self, or to the people that hurt you and wish them peace.

The Remains of Burning Therapeutic Journal

> I once sang of love
> and talked of freedom.
> Until I discovered,
> they are best lived.

Lauren Lott

Pain can show error. Write down ways you can show self-compassion when you discover you made the wrong decision or failed in some way.

The Remains of Burning Therapeutic Journal

I learnt to look
for little pops of joy,
instead of waiting
to be happy.

-how to change your life.

Lauren Lott

In the space below, write in detail, what you have noticed lately that has brought you joy.

(Once you start looking for joy you'll find it hard not to see it everywhere, even in the most ordinary of places.)

The Remains of Burning Therapeutic Journal

Watered by words.
Warmed by wonder,
the heart finds a way
to dissolve the pain.

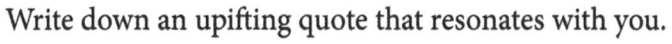

Write down an upifting quote that resonates with you.

What has stirred wonder in you recently? It could be a piece of art, something in nature, a poem, a story or a time in history. Write about what you found fasinating about it.

The Remains of Burning Therapeutic Journal

Awakened, I see burning bushes everywhere; in both the presence and absence of things hoped for.
And I, content to leave lost dreams, warm my heart over a new flame, and revel in the thought of living many lives in one lifetime.

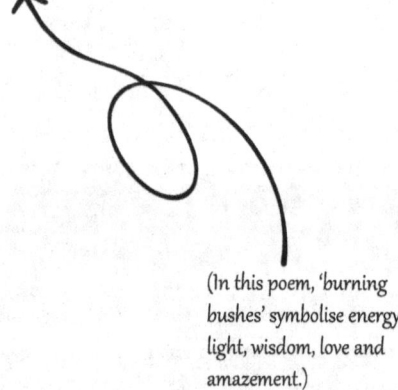

(In this poem, 'burning bushes' symbolise energy, light, wisdom, love and amazement.)

Lauren Lott

Write a note telling your past self one thing you know now that you didn't know then.

The Remains of Burning Therapeutic Journal

The first time I lost my leaves
I thought I was dying.
I waited all winter,
enduring the numb of midnight,
and frost at dawn,
until the sun started to set differently,
and the breeze began
to feel a little more hopeful.
I wish someone told me
life is a twisted coil
of beginnings and ends;
that living is changing,
and dying is a way
we each get to bless the earth.

Lauren Lott

Living is changing. Has dramatic change made you more or less afraid of what is in the future?

Write one thing you wish someone had told you about life.

And then I saw love relax.
Like it knew something
I couldn't grasp.
And I figured
it must be
bigger,
deeper,
wiser
than I had given credit.

Lauren Lott

Has pain shown you anything or anyone you have underestimated?

How do you relax?

The Remains of Burning Therapeutic Journal

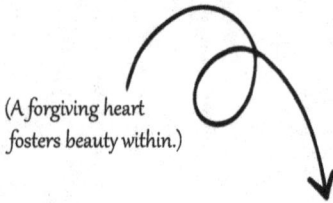

(A forgiving heart fosters beauty within.)

Forgiveness is the fairest of them all.

Lauren Lott

Who has forgiven you?

Who will you choose to forgive?

(Forgiveing others is like navigating a wild river. There is a lot of churn and tumble. At times it can be terrifying and seemingly impossible to master. Even though you may feel like you can never forgive, you can.)

Also By Lauren Lott

The Remains of Burning

A Strong and Fragile Thing.

Special Thanks

Thank you, dear reader, for your attention and trust. I hope the poems and writing prompts in this journal helped you journey towards wholeness and true inner freedom.

I understand that participating in this work means you have gone through significant pain and loss.

My heart is with you.

Connect with Me on

Instagram - @llott.writes
Tik Tok - @llott.writes
Facebook - @llott.writes

LOVE-MAIL

I'd love to pop some encouragement into your inbox.
Sign up at www.lauren-lott.com

I'd love to know what you thought of the journal.
An honest review would be appreciated.
Alternatively, contact me via my website (as above).

xx

Lauren Lott is the author of inspirational poetry books and journals.

In October 2020, Lauren's first collection 'The Remains of Burning' debuted on Amazon as the #1 New Release in Australian Poetry.

Her second collection, 'A Strong and Fragile Thing', was published in June 2021.

As a writer, poet and certified therapeutic writing couch, Lauren seeks to heal and enliven others through language. She believes the most rewarding life is found in practicing mindfulness and creativity.

Lauren lives in Lake Macquarie, Australia, with her family.

The Remains of Burning Therapeutic Journal

NOTES

Lauren Lott

NOTES

The Remains of Burning Therapeutic Journal

NOTES

Lauren Lott

NOTES

The Remains of Burning Therapeutic Journal

NOTES

Lauren Lott

NOTES

www.ingramcontent.com/pod-product-compliance
Lightning Source LLC
Chambersburg PA
CBHW010706020526
44107CB00082B/2697